101 FUNNY JOKES

VOLUME 2

THE HENNESSY KIDS

Featured Artwork by
KATHERINE HENNESSY

The Hennessy Entertainment
Company

101 Funny Jokes Volume 2 / by The Hennessy Kids

ISBN 978-1-989621-12-7 (Print)

ISBN 978-1-989621-13-4 (E-book)

1. Wit and humor, Juvenile. 2. English wit and humor. I. The Hennessy Kids, author.

The Hennessy Entertainment Company | HennessyEnt.com

To everybody who makes the fun stuff we enjoy.

1

A BUNCH OF JOKES

What kind of music do balloons hate?
    Pop music.

Did you hear about the claustrophobic astronaut?
    They just needed a little space.

Why are mountains so funny?
    They're just hill areas.

Why did Billy get cut when he fell on the grass?
    Because it's full of blades.

Why did the picture go to prison?
    Because it was framed.

.   .   .

Why do bicycles fall over?
  Because they're two-tired.

Why was the broom late?
  It over-swept.

Where do sailboats go when they're sick?
  To the dock.

What kind of water can't freeze?
  Hot water.

Why didn't the shopper buy the camo pants they wanted?
  They couldn't find any.

What did the family say when they lost 25% of their roof?
  Oof.

Why are elevator jokes so good?
  They work on many levels.

What do you call a boomerang that doesn't come back?
  A stick.

Why are balloons so expensive?
  Inflation.

                    .   .   .

Why was the calendar afraid?
    Its days were numbered.

What do kids do during recess on rainy days?
    Play bored games.

What's blue and smells like red paint?
    Blue paint.

What's red and bad for your teeth?
    A brick.

What did the zero say to the eight?
    Nice belt.

What has ears but cannot hear?
    A cornfield.

Can February March?
    No, but April May.

What building in New York has the most stories?
    The New York Public Library.

Why did it get so hot in the stadium after the game?
    All the fans left.

.   .   .

What do you call a can opener that doesn't work?
    A can't opener.

Why do we tell actors to "break a leg?"
    Because every play has a cast.

Why did the lawyer show up in court in his underwear?
    He forgot his lawsuit.

How did the beauty school student do on her manicure test?
    She nailed it.

Why did the genie get mad?
    Because he was rubbed the wrong way.

What should you wear to a tea party?
    A t-shirt.

What's rain's favorite accessory?
    A rainbow.

Where does a sink go dancing?
    The dish-co .

What's the most popular video game at the bread makers?
    Knead for Speed.

. . .

What do you get if Santa goes down the chimney while the fire is lit?

Crisp Kringle.

Why is a cemetery a great place to write a story?

Because there are so many plots there.

Why was the equal sign so humble?

Because it wasn't greater than or less than anyone else.

Are any Halloween monsters good at math?

No - unless you Count Dracula.

How can you make a tissue dance?

Put a little boogie in it.

What do you call a train with a cold?

A-choo choo train.

How did the barber win the race?

They knew a short cut.

How do you talk to a giant?

Use big words.

What did the meteorologist say when they tried to catch fog?

I mist.

. . .

Why did the cell phone get glasses?
>Because it lost all its contacts.

What runs around a baseball field but never moves?
>A fence.

What musical instrument can you find in the bathroom?
>A tuba toothpaste.

Why do bees have sticky hair?
>They use honeycombs.

What do you call a droid that likes taking the scenic route?
>R2-Detour.

Why is Cinderella so bad at playing football?
>She runs away from the ball.

How do billboards talk to one another?
>With sign language.

Why did Humpty Dumpty have a great fall?
>To make up for his terrible summer.

What did the little boat say to the yacht?
>"Can I interest you in a little row-mance?"

. . .

Where do twins go on vacation?
    Pair-is.

I'm not mad that someone stole my flashlight.
    I'm delighted.

A ride on a hot air balloon might not be the most incredible thing ever, but it is up there.

My dad told me to get a new job skill, so I learned lockpicking.
    It's opened a lot of doors for me.

Teachers love white boards. They are remarkable.

My friend didn't understand cloning.
    I said that makes two of us.

2

CREATURE JOKES

What did the farmer call the cow that had no milk?
  An udder failure.

Why are spiders so smart?
  They can find everything on the web.

What's worse than finding a worm in your apple?
  Finding half a worm in your apple.

What do you call bears with no ears?
  B.

Why couldn't the pony talk?
  Because she was just a little hoarse.

                    . . .

How do you keep a bull from charging?
    Cancel its credit card.

Why did the pig have ink all over his face?
    Because he just came out of the pen.

What do you get from a pampered cow?
    Spoiled milk.

What do you call a hen who counts her eggs?
    A mathema-chicken.

What kind of lion doesn't roar?
    A dandelion.

What is black and white and red all over?
    A zebra with a sunburn.

What kind of music do whales like?
    They listen to the orca-stra.

What kind of jobs do funny chickens have?
    They are comedy-hens.

What's the strongest type of sea creature?
    Mussels.

                        .   .   .

What's a kitty cat's favorite color?
   Purr-ple.

What kind of photos will you find on a turtle's phone?
   Shell-fies.

What's a bee's normal haircut?
   A buzz cut.

What do you get when you cross a centipede with a parrot?
   A walkie talkie.

What do you call an illegally parked amphibian?
   Toad.

What do you get when you cross a porcupine with a snail?
   A slowpoke.

What breed of dog can jump higher than a skyscraper?
   Any breed of dog. Skyscrapers can't jump.

What do you call a cow that can't moo?
   A milk dud.

What do snakes like to study in school?
   Hissss-tory.

. . .

What did the frog order for lunch?
    A burger and a croak.

What do cows order from?
    Cattle-logs.

What creature is smarter than a talking parrot?
    A spelling bee.

What's black and white and red all over?
    A sunburned zebra.

What did the snail say when it rode on the turtle's back?
    Wheeeee.

Where do sheep go to get their hair cut?
    The baa-baa shop.

Which bird is always out of breath?
    A puffin.

3

ARTWORK

What kind of music do balloons hate? Pop music.

Why are mountains so funny? They are hill areas.

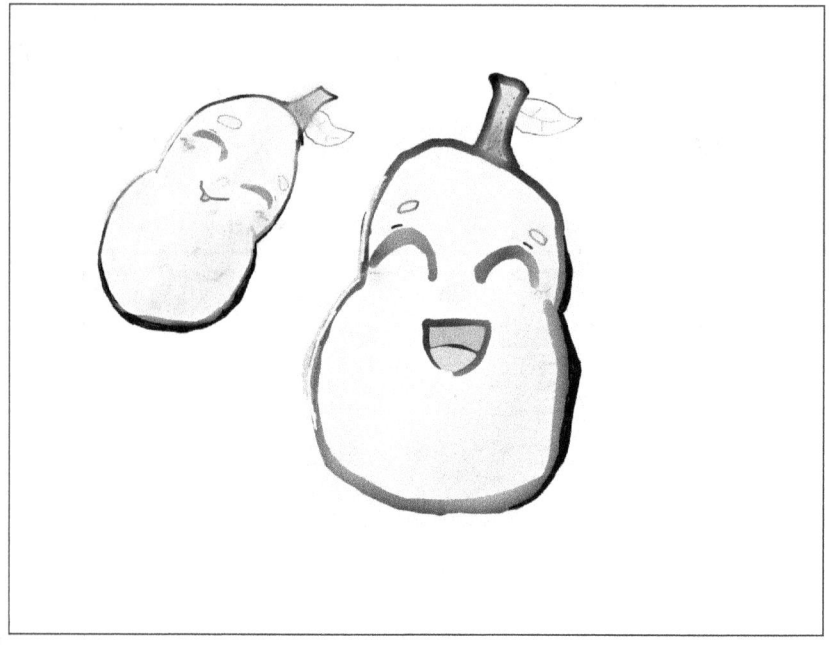

What kind of fruit do twins love the most? Pears.

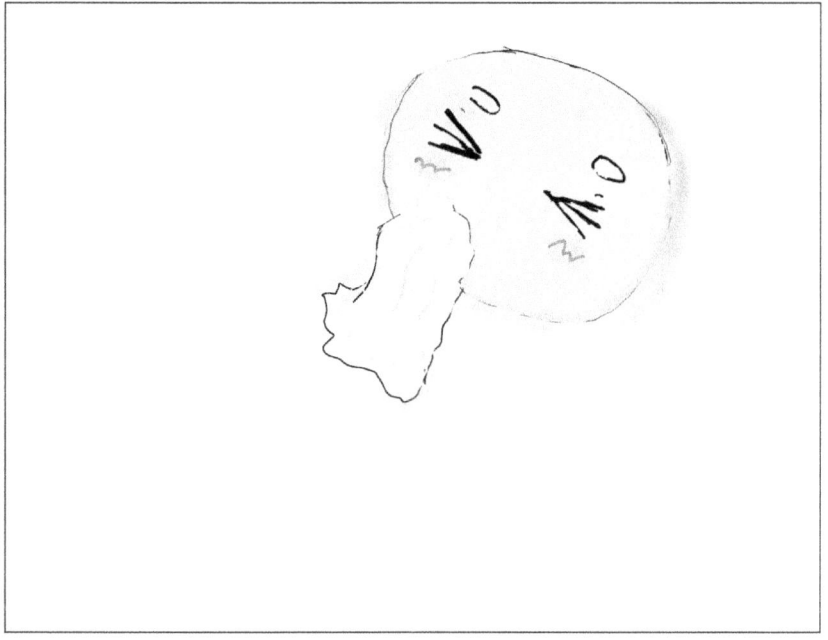

How can you make a tissue dance? Put a little boogie in it.

4

TASTY JOKES

How does a cucumber become a pickle?
    It goes through a jarring experience.

Why oranges wear sunscreen?
    So they don't peel.

Why did the student eat his homework?
    Because his teacher said it was a piece of cake.

Why do we put candles on top of birthday cakes?
    Because it's hard to light them from the bottom.

What do you call a retired vegetable?
    A has-bean.

· · ·

Why did the baker put the cake in the freezer?
    She wanted to ice it.

Where do you learn to make banana splits?
    At sundae school.

What kind of fruit do twins love the most?
    Pears.

What do they serve for breakfast on flights?
    Plane bagels.

What do cowboys put on their salads?
    Ranch dressing.

Where do hamburgers go dancing?
    A meat ball.

What kind of vegetable is angry?
    A steamed carrot.

What vegetable do sailors never want on their boats?
    Leeks.

5

SCHOOL JOKES

Why did the teacher draw on the window?
    Because he wanted his lesson to be very clear.

What's a pirate's favorite class to take in school?
    Arrrt.

What did the school librarian say when a book fell on their head?
    I have only my shelf to blame.

How did the student feel when he learned about electricity?
    Totally shocked.

Why did the bikes get detention at school?
    They spoke too much.

. . .

Why didn't anyone want to eat next to the basketball team?
Because they dribble too much.

6

ACTIVITIES

READY TO GIVE YOUR MIND
A WORKOUT?

HERE IS A MAZE,
A NUMBER PUZZLE,
AND A WORD SEARCH
FOR FUN!

NUMBER PUZZLE

			6
	1	0	6
3		5	11
3			9
11	7	8	11

Missing numbers are between 0 to 9.
The numbers in each row add up to total on right.
The numbers in each column add up to total on bottom.
The diagonal numbers also add up to boxes on right side.

WORD SEARCH

```
F T U E S M Y K H E S W B G D
L R C R E C R V I V P E W M T
D D A O T B A N Z Z I Y J C F
Q E A M W F E Q E I D I C R C
P V C M E G P B C W E P Q M A
S C K W H D R L O B R N W Y U
Z X C C F A B R I V Q G W Q T
F A K Z I H M O P Z H I E A L
W E L P T R Q D O O B S K P C
C A R R O T B O L G N M A S V
E Q I C C K W C I A I Y C G Z
B A L L O O N K O A D E N N C
L X U J Z T U C N A M T A A Y
O C C E Q U A L Y Y S M M I Q
S F P I D H K C I T S O B S Y
```

BALLOON	BRICK	SPIDER	PEARS
FRAMED	SIGN	WORM	CARROT
DOCK	GENIE	TOAD	PONY
CAMO	EQUAL	BEE	LION
STICK	BOOGIE	CAKE	ZEBRA

7

YOUR FAVOURITE JOKE

What is your favourite knock knock joke that isn't in this book?

Send it to us at thehennessykids@gmail.com, and we'll look to share it online with all our friends.

ACKNOWLEDGMENTS

Special thank you to everybody who is getting our joke books out from their public library and then sharing jokes with their family and friends!

Thank you for reading our book! We hope you enjoyed it. Please tell these jokes to your friends and family and make more people happy.

ABOUT THE AUTHORS

The Hennessy Kids think the world would be better with more smiles.

Want to know when our new books and games are available? Sign up for our newsletter or visit www.hennessyent.com!

BOOKS BY THE HENNESSY KIDS

101 Funny Jokes, Vol. 1

101 Funny Jokes, Vol. 2

101 Pet Jokes

101 Knock Knock Jokes, Vol. 1

101 Knock Knock Jokes, Vol. 2

101 Knock Knock Jokes, Vol. 3

The Big Book Of Jokes

101 Nature Jokes

101 Food Jokes

101 Halloween Jokes

101 Christmas Jokes

101 School Jokes

Visit hennessyent.com for the complete up-to-date list of our books and games!

www.ingramcontent.com/pod-product-compliance
Lightning Source LLC
Chambersburg PA
CBHW070948120626
46546CB00004B/1617